MARTIN LUTHER KING, JR.

by **Herb Boyd**

illustrations by **Pablo Marcos**

ABDO
Publishing Company

HEROES OF AMERICA™

Edited by
Joshua Hanft and Rochelle Larkin

visit us at
www.abdopub.com

Library edition published in 2005 by ABDO Publishing Company, 4940 Viking Drive, Suite 622, Edina, Minnesota 55435. Published by agreement with Playmore Incorporated Publishers and Waldman Publishing Corporation.

Cover art, interior art, and text copyright © 1990 by Playmore Incorporated Publishers and Waldman Publishing Corporation, New York, New York.

International copyrights reserved in all countries. No part of this book may be reproduced in any form without written permission from the publisher.

Printed in the United States.

Library of Congress Cataloging-in-Publication Data

Boyd, Herb, 1938-
    Martin Luther King, Jr. / by Herb Boyd ; illustrations by Pablo Marcos. -- Library ed.
      p. cm. -- (Heroes of America)
    Originally published: New York : Baronet Books, c1996.
    ISBN 1-59679-258-2
    1. King, Martin Luther, Jr., 1929-1968--Juvenile literature. 2. African
Americans--Biography--Juvenile literature. 3. Civil rights workers--United
States--Biography--Juvenile literature. 4. Baptists--United
States--Clergy--Biography--Juvenile literature. I. Marcos, Pablo, ill. II. Title. III. Series.

E185.97.K5B68 2005
323'.092--dc22
[B]

                                        2004062306

Table of Contents

Important Dates

1929 Martin Luther King, Jr. born in Atlanta

1944 Martin enters Morehouse College

1947 Martin is ordained as minister

1951 Martin graduates from Crozer
        Theological Seminary

1953 Martin and Coretta Scott are married

1955 The Montgomery Alabama bus
        boycott begins

1960 Sit-in demonstrations begin

1961 Freedom rides begin

1963 March on Washington

1964 Martin wins the Nobel Peace Prize

1965 Voting Rights bill becomes law

1968 Martin makes "I've been to the
        mountain top" speech

1968 Martin Luther King, Jr. is killed
        in Memphis

Chapter 1

Coming of Age in Atlanta

Each of the kindergarten students was eager to answer the teacher's question. But as usual, the hand of the slender little boy in the middle row was first in the air. He was even quicker to respond than his older sister, Christine, who sat in the front row.

"Well, M.L., tell us what you'd like to be when you grow up," the teacher said.

"I want to be a preacher like my father and my grandfather, so I can use big words like they do," the boy replied.

"I Want to Be a Preacher."

MARTIN LUTHER KING, JR.

"You do like to use big words, don't you, Martin?" the teacher said.

"Yes, ma'am. I learned how to spell another one the other day from my grandmother. Rambunctious. I'll spell it for you. R-A-M-B-U-N-C-T-I-O-U-S. She always calls me that."

"And what does it mean?" the teacher asked.

"My grandmother says it's a word to describe somebody who can't keep still and is always busy getting into something."

Just as Martin Luther King, Jr. finished his reply, the school bell rang. "Okay, children," the teacher said, "gather your books and I'll see you all tomorrow. And try not to be too rambunctious!"

The children laughed and several of them crowded around Martin, slapping him on the back. Martin gathered up his crayons and coloring book, tucked them neatly into his school bag, and marched out of the room and down the hall with his sister.

One by one their friends said good-bye and went off in different directions. Martin liked the praise they had given him, but they were keeping him from hurrying home. His mother had promised to take him shopping for a new pair of pants and a shirt. On Sunday he was going to be baptized at his father's church.

Martin had asked to be baptized because Christine recently had been, and whatever Christine did, five-year-old Martin was right behind her. He had even pestered his parents to allow him to attend Yonge Elementary School with Christine, a year ahead of schedule.

It was a little chilly for September in Atlanta as Martin and Christine walked home down the tree-lined street. Although Christine was sixteen months

Martin and Christine Walked Home.

older than Martin, they were about the same size. When they turned onto Auburn Street they were in step, side by side, but a few doors from their large Victorian house, Martin suddenly began to run. Christine took off after him, but Martin was through the front door and into the house by the time she reached the porch.

As soon as the door slammed behind Christine, their youngest brother, A.D., came down the stairs. Martin glanced at the old grandfather clock. He and Christine had made it home from school in ten minutes.

"Who's keeping up all that fuss out there?" Grandmother Williams called, coming in from the kitchen. Grandmother Williams was a proud, proper woman whom the children called Mama. They called their own mother Mother Dear.

"Go and wash your hands," said Grandmother

Williams firmly. "There are cups of hot chocolate on the table for both of you. How did it go at school today?"

"Mama, M.L. told the teacher about that word you always use," Christine reported. "You know, rambunctious."

"For goodness sake," Grandmother Williams exclaimed, drying her hands on her apron. "Guess I better watch what I say around here."

After drinking his hot chocolate, Martin went to his room to read while he waited for his mother to get home. He took his favorite book of Bible stories from the shelf and sprawled across the bed. The illustrated book had stories about Daniel in the lion's den, Moses parting the Red Sea and Noah building the ark.

Martin liked best the stories about people overcoming great odds. He never tired of looking at the

He Would Imitate His Father.

pictures of Samson defeating an army with only the jawbone of an ass, or David bringing down Goliath with a rock and his slingshot. Sometimes young Martin would dream about being as strong as Samson and as courageous as David.

Martin enjoyed listening to his father preach about these Bible heroes at Ebenezer Baptist Church. It seemed as if his father could make the biblical characters almost come alive during his sermons. And many a time, after coming home from church, Martin would stand in front of the mirror and imitate his father, deepening his voice to match his father's powerful way of speaking. "One day I'm gonna stand in the pulpit," young Martin would often tell his brother and sister, "just like Daddy and Granddaddy."

Young Martin, or M.L., as everyone called him, was proud of his father and grandfather, and he made up his mind that he wanted to be just like them. He had seen and been told what great preachers his father and grandfather were. He spent many hours studying, pretending he was his father, and getting ready for the pulpit.

His grandfather, the Reverend A.D. Williams, his mother's father, was a good storyteller. Little Martin and his brother and sister spent hours at Grandfather's feet, trying to keep up with his rolling voice and wonderful imagination.

Grandfather Williams often told the family about his growing up as a slave-preacher's son, and how he later had run away from home to seek his fortune. He never told them why he had run away, and no one asked—not even the adults. Later, when Martin was older, he guessed that his grandfather must have been rambunctious too—always ready to try something new—and that was why he had run

At Grandfather's Feet

away. It was hard to ask a question anyway, once Grandfather started telling his stories.

He often told about his college days. The Reverend Williams was one of the three black men to be awarded Morehouse College's first diplomas, in 1897. In the bedroom upstairs there was a picture of Grandfather dressed in a long waistcoat with a high-collar shirt, his eyes seemingly fixed on the future. "I'm one of the original Morehouse men!" Martin's grandfather was fond of saying.

Martin's mother, Alberta, sometimes tried to hush her father when he began telling the children stories about when she was a little girl. "Of course, she wasn't as noisy as the three of you," he would say with a grin. "I guess you can say she was a very quiet and serious child. Still water runs deep, as the saying goes."

When Reverend Williams talked about Martin's

father, and about how he first began dating his daughter, it was Martin's father who would always try to change the subject. "I think they really started getting serious about the time I was building a new church," Pastor Williams would recall. "When your father convinced John Hope, who was then the president of Morehouse, to allow him to study there, I knew your father was the man who was worthy of my daughter."

Martin, Sr. was a hardworking man, and always had a lot of good ideas. As a preacher he knew how to keep his listeners wide awake and interested in what he had to say. Nobody was a better organizer. Martin, Sr. was soon the leader of one of the most prominent churches in town.

Young Martin's religious faith, like much of his character, came to him from his strong, loving family. The family both protected him and taught him

The Clerk Would Not Wait on Them.

to be good—a Christian who believed that the welfare of others was more important than his personal needs.

One of the most unforgettable examples Martin was given as a child was his father's active opposition to racism and unfair treatment of black people. Martin's father refused to ride the city buses, or obey the laws that segregated, or separated, black people from white people. There were many such laws at that time.

Martin often witnessed his father's refusal to follow these unfair laws their city imposed. One day Martin and his father were shopping in a shoe store when a sales clerk told them he could not wait on them because they were sitting in an area reserved for whites only.

"I'll be happy to wait on you if you'll move to those seats in the rear," the sales clerk said politely.

MARTIN LUTHER KING, JR.

"There's nothing wrong with these seats," Martin's father responded. "We're quite comfortable here."

"Sorry," said the clerk, "but you'll have to move."

"We'll either buy shoes sitting here," Martin's father said firmly, "or we won't buy shoes at all." He grabbed Martin's hand and they walked out of the store. Martin, Sr. was fuming with anger.

"I don't care how long they have had this system. I will never accept it," Martin, Sr. said, squeezing his son's hand as they hurried down the street.

During another incident, this time with a police officer, Martin's father once again stood up to a white man. Martin, Sr. had accidentally driven past a stop sign when a policeman in a patrol car pulled alongside them.

"All right, boy—pull over and let me see your license," the officer demanded.

"I Will Never Accept It."

MARTIN LUTHER KING, JR.

"I'm no boy. This is a boy," Martin, Sr. said, pointing to his son. "I'm a man, and until you address me as one, I will not listen to you."

The policeman was so shocked, he wrote up a ticket nervously and left the scene as quickly as possible.

This example was not wasted on young Martin. He refused to drink from water fountains marked "For Coloreds Only," nor would he attend the Jim Crow movie houses where, because of the so-called Jim Crow standards, blacks had to enter and leave through a rear door. This was quite a sacrifice for a ten-year-old who had heard all the excitement about a recent film called *Gone With The Wind*.

Like his father, he simply could not accept separate waiting rooms, eating places, and rest rooms for black people—not only because "separate" always meant unequal, he said, but "because the very idea of separation did something to my sense of dignity and self-respect."

By the time he was twelve years old, though, Martin had to set aside some of these feelings for a while. As a seventh-grader, Martin enrolled in the Atlanta University Laboratory School, and in order to get there each morning he had to ride a segregated city bus. There was no other choice and Martin wanted to attend this school. There were exciting classes there and Martin first began to study the violin and later the piano.

His favorite subjects were history and English—and he excelled. All those big words he had memorized—some from his father's sermons, but mostly from a radio show called *Seven Minutes at the Mike*—were put to good use. He also enjoyed discussions about religion. But after his first year at the Lab School, his faith was once more tested.

23

He Loved to Watch the Musicians.

MARTIN LUTHER KING, JR.

One Sunday in May, Martin heard there was going to be a parade downtown. He was so excited that he pushed his homework aside and sneaked out of the house. He hurried off to see the military uniforms and to hear the marching music. He loved to watch the long rows of prancing musicians with their horns gleaming in the sun. Some high-stepping girls twirling batons had just passed by when one of Martin's friends ran up to him all out of breath.

"M.L., your grandmother is sick!" his friend yelled over the sound of bass drums. "I think she had a heart attack."

Martin rushed home to learn that Mama had died. She had died while waiting to speak at a Women's Day event at Mount Olive Baptist church. Martin was overwhelmed with sadness and anger—angry at himself for sneaking off without permission, to satisfy his own curiosity.

For many weeks he blamed himself for Mama's death, convinced that she would still be alive had he not run off to enjoy a parade. This sadness lingered, and caused Martin to question his belief in God. He would be a college student before he started believing again—but never, after rediscovering his faith, would he be a "doubting Martin" again.

He Blamed Himself.

Chapter 2

The Making of a Minister

For the next two years, Martin, now called "Tweedie" because of his fondness for tweed suits, worked and studied very hard. He finished high school when he was just fifteen. Now he was ready to attend Morehouse, the college his father and grandfather had attended.

Although now officially a college student, Martin could not decide what his major course of study would be. Martin began Morehouse with the idea of being a doctor, but the study of biology didn't appeal to him, nor was he very interested in law. Before long, though, his faith and his old dreams came back to him. He knew then what his life's work was to be.

Martin's decision to become a minister pleased his father. Martin, Sr. announced the news to his congregation and told them that his son would soon deliver his trial sermon.

Worried about this first sermon at Ebenezer, Martin studied the works of several great speakers, including Harry Emerson Fosdick's "Life Is What You Make It." There were also long hours reading Henry David Thoreau's *Essay on Civil Disobedience.* This great book was Martin's introduction to the idea of nonviolent resistance, so critical to the philosophy of the leader he was to become.

When the time came for Martin to preach, there was already a huge crowd gathered in anticipation

Giving the Senior Sermon

of his sermon. The sermon had to be moved from the basement to the church's sanctuary. At first Martin was nervous, but after a sentence or two he became more confident. The now-famous deep, soothing tone of his later sermons was not yet fully developed at this time; even so, his voice was stronger than that of most boys his age. And Martin used just enough big words to impress the large congregation—and his father, who made him the church's assistant pastor.

Martin was such a good student in college, he was chosen to give the Senior Sermon. Showing the same confidence he had summoned up for his first preaching at Ebenezer, Martin moved this audience too, with his marvelous sermon. For years afterward, many people who were there would recall Martin's sermon and many told him they knew even then that one day he would be a great man.

MARTIN LUTHER KING, JR.

In the summer of 1948, Martin and Christine graduated in separate ceremonies. Martin then decided to enroll at Crozer Theological Seminary in Chester, Pennsylvania—a racially mixed school noted for its high academic standards. It took only a few classes for Martin to decide to study theology seriously.

The courses at Crozer were not easy, but Martin did very well. He studied many of the great thinkers and philosophers, such as Rousseau, Hobbes, and the Christian theologist Reinhold Niebuhr. Of the eleven black students who entered that summer, Martin earned the highest grades. He was well on his way to being the valedictorian of his class.

Among the most influential of his teachers was Walter Rauschenbusch. Martin was deeply impressed by Rauschenbusch's emphasis on the Social Gospel, which meant using one's faith and

He Studied Many of the Great Thinkers.

belief in righteousness to correct social wrongs.

As a student Martin distinguished himself as a speaker, using the style and technique of Professor Robert Keighton, who introduced him to the works of Shakespeare, T.S. Eliot and St. Augustine. In these classes Martin learned all about public speaking and how to use his voice effectively. He completed his days at Crozer as the top student and set his sights on graduate school at Boston University.

With the best wishes of his friends and recommendations from the faculty at Crozer, Martin packed his new car for the long drive from Atlanta to Boston.

There was a brief stop in Brooklyn where he preached a guest sermon at the Reverend Gardner Taylor's Concord Baptist Church, one of the largest Protestant congregations in the United States. Because Martin's father was a friend of Reverend

MARTIN LUTHER KING, JR.

Taylor and both preachers were members of the National Baptist Convention, Martin was given this special invitation. At twenty-two, it was an opportunity that few young ministers ever dreamed of, and Martin made the most of it, his powerful words inspiring his listeners to stand up and applaud.

Two days later, after the excitement at Concord, Martin was back in the classroom. Boston University, with its busy campus in the heart of the city, felt very hectic after the small, quiet atmosphere of Crozer.

Martin was studying philosophy. There was a mountain of books to read and lots of homework. There were so many assignments to complete that it left little time for him to get involved in campus activities. Instead of protesting the Korean War or joining the efforts by students to integrate a clerks'

Martin Met Coretta.

union at Sears, Martin worked in his room or studied in the library. Although Martin would later become a great leader, none of the student papers he wrote during his years at Boston University had anything to do with civil rights.

However, there was one thing that, now and then, kept him from his books—a girlfriend. Martin met Coretta Scott in 1952 and it was almost love at first sight. Coretta, two years older than Martin, was from Alabama, and a graduate of Antioch College in Ohio. Coretta was in Boston studying voice at the New England Conservatory of Music. She was very pretty—Martin spent as much time as he could with her.

"The four things that I look for in a wife are character, intelligence, personality and beauty," Martin told Coretta one day, "and you have all of those things." They were both good students. They would finish all their homework before going to a movie or taking a walk in the park.

Martin had chosen his future wife, but would she impress his father and his mother? Only after several meetings was Martin's family convinced he was serious about Coretta. When he insisted that she would be his wife, the family supported his wishes. They were married June 18, 1953.

Coretta knew she had married a man who could become a great and important leader, and she believed that she would be worthy of him. But she was also determined to have her say, no matter what Martin thought. During their marriage ceremony, Coretta insisted that the promise to "obey" her husband be left out of the wedding vows. She was determined that their marriage be one of equality. Coretta and Martin agreed that what was good for one was good for the other, and the two were

They Were Married in 1953.

married.

"The next place is bound to have a vacancy," Martin assured Coretta as it began to get dark. He switched on the headlights. "There has to be one hotel room left on the way to Georgia!"

"I hadn't planned on spending our wedding night driving around in the car," Coretta said with a laugh.

"I know," Martin answered. "Me either."

After what seemed like hours of driving, Martin pulled into the parking lot of a small building with a neatly-kept lawn and garden. Coretta peered out the car window. "Where are we?" she asked.

Then she saw a small sign. It was already dark, and Coretta squinted to read the sign in the dim light of a streetlamp. "But, Martin," she gasped. "It's a funeral parlor! Why are we stopping here?"

It wasn't just any old place—it was the funeral

parlor of a friend, and rather than drive all night, Martin and Coretta cheerfully ended up spending their wedding night there.

"Well," Coretta whispered as they turned out the lights, "we decided what's good for one is good for the other. And besides—how many folks get to spend their wedding night in a funeral parlor?"

Martin laughed. With an ability to adapt to any situation, to laugh at silly things, and ponder serious questions, Coretta was ideally suited for Martin, as was he for her. Their marriage was off to a good start.

A year later, Martin accepted a call to become the minister at Dexter Avenue Baptist Church, in Montgomery, Alabama. Coretta was not happy. She didn't want to move back to the South where racial laws still prevented black Americans from living as

"My Calling is from God."

they pleased. But things were just slowly, too slowly, starting to change. One of the crucial laws of segregation that had existed for years came to an end soon after Coretta and Martin returned to Montgomery—the Supreme Court ruled in the historic *Brown v. Board of Education of Topeka* case, that racial segregation in public schools was unconstitutional.

When Martin arrived at Dexter, he began changing things in the same way his father had done when he had taken over Ebenezer. In his opening sermon as the new pastor, Martin let it be known that he was in charge.

"I believe that my calling to this church is from God," he said in a letter to the church. "If God has appointed me to this task, then what man has a right to challenge the decision?" Martin quickly formed new committees, boards, and councils. He was like a new broom, many church members said— and he was sweeping things clean.

Despite a church and community schedule that would have worn out the average man, Martin still found time to complete work on his doctorate degree at Boston, which meant making several trips to the campus. These final demands of studying for his Ph.D. were not easy, and Martin had to learn about a number of difficult religious ideas.

He was also deeply concerned about the growing racial problems in Montgomery. Those problems worsened after fifteen-year-old Claudette Colvin was snatched from a bus and jailed because she refused to get up and give her seat to a white passenger.

"My father would never tolerate this," Martin told Coretta sadly. "Something has to be done."

"What will you do now, Martin?"

Deeply Concerned About Racial Problems

MARTIN LUTHER KING, JR.

"We need to organize," Martin answered. "There's strength in numbers. We need to get together and stand up for our civil rights."

Not long afterward, it became clear that Martin was right. The time for change had come. Colvin's situation was only the beginning—the real test case against the city's racial injustice was just around the bend.

Chapter Three

The Montgomery Bus Boycott

"When I got off from work that evening of December 1, 1955," Rosa Parks, a black woman, wrote in her memoir, "I went to Court Square as usual to catch the Cleveland Avenue bus home. I didn't look to see who was driving when I got on, and by the time I recognized him, I had already paid my fare. It was the same driver who had put me off the bus back in 1943.... I saw a vacant seat in the middle section of the bus and took it."

Parks sat down and refused to move from the

"I Saw a Vacant Seat and Took It."

section reserved for whites. The driver threatened her, but she persisted, and refused to move. "Eventually two policemen came," Parks continued. "They got on the bus, and one of them asked me why I didn't stand up. I asked him, 'Why do you all push us around?' He said to me, and I quote him exactly, 'Don't know, but the law is the law and you're under arrest.'"

These are the simple circumstances that launched the great civil rights movement of the 1960s. "People always say that I didn't give up my seat because I was tired," Parks explains, "but that wasn't true. I was not tired physically, or no more tired than I usually was at the end of the working day. I was not old, although some people have the image of me as being old then. I was forty-two. No, the only tired I was, was tired of giving in."

Parks also explains in her memoir that her act

was not planned in advance, as many people think. "People have asked me if it occurred to me then that I could be the test case the National Association for the Advancement of Colored People (NAACP) had been looking for. I did not think about that at all. In fact, if I had let myself think too deeply about what might happen to me, I might have gotten off the bus. But I chose to remain." Her cup of endurance, as Martin would say later, "had merely run over."

Rosa Parks spent a few hours in jail. After she was released, E.D. Nixon, of the Montgomery NAACP, asked her if she would be willing to make her incident a test case against segregation. Parks agreed, and within a couple of days a support committee was formed. Martin, who had received his Ph.D. from Boston University that spring, quickly joined the committee.

The committee members, including the Reverend

Rosa Parks Spent a Few Hours in Jail.

MARTIN LUTHER KING, JR.

Ralph Abernathy of First Baptist Church, who was Martin's good friend, decided that a boycott of the bus company was the best way to express their outrage at the unfairness of segregation. Following a citywide meeting four days after Rosa Parks was arrested, the committee hammered out a statement that would be its first leaflet:

- Don't ride the bus to work, to town, to school, or any place—Monday, December 5. Another Negro woman has been arrested and put in jail because she refused to give up her bus seat.
- Don't ride the buses to work, to town, to school, or anywhere on Monday. If you work, take a cab, or share a ride, or walk.
- Come to a mass meeting, Monday at 7 p.m., at the Holt Street Baptist Church for further instructions.

MARTIN LUTHER KING, JR.

It was late at night when Martin finally arrived home. He was worn out from the long meetings and endless discussion about what should be done.

"You look tired, Martin," Coretta said softly, helping him off with his jacket. "Come and eat something."

Coretta and Martin went into the kitchen and set out a few things for a light snack together. "It's too late for dinner," Martin said. "I don't think I could eat that much, anyway."

"What's wrong?" Coretta asked. "Didn't things go well today?"

The committee Martin had so eagerly joined had done its job of spreading the word and alerting the community, but Martin still wondered if people would have the courage to carry out the boycott of the bus company.

"People have to be strong," Martin said. "It's going

"People Will Follow Your Example."

to take a lot of guts to see this boycott to the end. People can't afford to get weak and give up. I just hope they're up to the task. It's only just begun."

"That's where you can help them," Coretta said. "People will follow your example. With your guidance, people will learn to be strong."

Around midnight, Martin received a call telling him that the Negro taxi company in Montgomery would support the protest by carrying passengers; even so, Martin was concerned about the outcome of their plan.

But that morning, when Martin stumbled out of bed before six, still weary from the previous day's activity, he was in for a great surprise. Living only a few feet from a bus stop, Martin and Coretta could see how many passengers were aboard each bus. Martin and Coretta waited anxiously for the arrival of the first bus. While he was in the kitchen getting another cup of coffee, Coretta called to him:

"Martin, Martin, come quickly," she said. "The bus is empty!"

He was astonished. The South Jackson Bus line was one of the busiest in the city, and the buses were normally packed. Martin and Coretta were overjoyed. Their excitement increased with each empty bus that passed.

How is the boycott working in other parts of the city? Martin wondered. He drove all over town to find out. Soon Martin discovered that the boycott was more than he had hoped for—the black residents from nearly every part of the city were taking part in the protest.

Meanwhile, later that morning, Rosa Parks was scheduled to stand trial. After the judge heard the arguments, he found Parks guilty of disobeying a city ordinance and fined her ten dollars. Martin

"The Bus Is Empty!"

knew that the decision would be likely to alarm the community further, and move them to positive action. He was right.

"We need something more than a committee," Martin told a group of supporters. "It is time to form a solid organization." And as soon as the organization was formed, Martin was nominated to be the president of the group, which took the name proposed by the Reverend Abernathy—the Montgomery Improvement Association (MIA). Now they had a strong organization and leader.

But while Martin looked forward to his leadership role, he was also concerned about what it would demand of him. He was very nervous as he thought about his first speech before the association. At last, with little time to prepare, Martin put the matter in the hands of the Lord. *Open your mouth and God will speak for you,* he said to himself.

And open his mouth he did. He talked about Parks's experience, the long years of mistreatment in the city, and the need to continue the nonviolent protest. "If you will protest courageously and yet with dignity and Christian love," he said toward the end of his speech, "when the history books are written in future generations, the historians will have to pause and say, 'There lived a great people—a black people—who injected new meaning and dignity into the veins of civilization.'"

He sat down to tremendous applause. Martin, soon to be the major figure in the civil rights movement, was now ready to lead the march toward freedom and equality for all.

As the boycott gathered steam, there were a number of problems to solve. Getting people back and forth to work could not depend on hit-or-miss arrangements; transportation had to go smoothly.

Money Came in from All Over.

The various committees of the MIA took on this task. Pickup and delivery operations were devised.

Money was urgently needed, too. Funds were needed to keep the car pools running. Some money came from preachers who donated their fees from guest sermons at churches in and out of the city. And soon money began to come in from all over the nation, and even from Europe and Asia.

Three weeks passed by and the deadlock between the boycotters and the bus company continued. Neither side was willing to surrender an inch. Each meeting was conducted amid bitter disagreement with representatives from the bus company charging Martin and the MIA with breaking the law. There were also accusations that the MIA had some members who were communists. People opposed to the MIA accused them of disturbing a quiet community, and causing unrest among neighbors who had lived together peacefully before.

One white resident told Martin the boycott had set race relations back several years and had ended what had been a peaceful coexistence.

"Sir," Martin replied, "you have never had a real peace in Montgomery. You have had a sort of negative peace in which the Negro too often accepted his state of subordination. But this is not true peace.

"True peace is not merely the absence of tension; it is the presence of justice. The tension we see in Montgomery today is the necessary tension that comes when the oppressed rise up and start to move forward toward a permanent, positive peace."

Unable to break the boycott, the bus company told lies, tried all kinds of tricks, and misled the media. False rumors were spread that the boycott was over. Black residents were harassed by other city agencies, and then came the death threats to

"You Never Had Real Peace."

the leaders of the MIA.

On January 30, while Martin was addressing a meeting about the importance of nonviolence and direct action, he was told that his house had been bombed.

He rushed home to find that an explosion had burst on the porch. Coretta and their baby daughter, Yolanda, were all right, though a bit shaken. Someone had also thrown sticks of dynamite on E.D. Nixon's lawn. The showdown was now at a new and dangerous level.

With the spread of violence, Martin and the entire city of Montgomery were placed in the national spotlight, and the young minister was caught up in a spin of speaking engagements that took him and his cause all across the country. But soon all the traveling and meetings took their toll, and Martin's doctor told him to slow down and take it easy, or he would damage his health.

Martin intended to take it easy, but then another problem came up. The city's attorneys were going to call the car pool a public nuisance operating without a license. A court order against the car pool would make transportation for the boycotters most difficult. With winter coming on, the protesters would be forced back to the buses. It was a desperate moment, and once more Martin placed the crisis in the hands of his Lord. "He can make a way out of no way," he preached.

On November 13, almost a year after the boycott began, Martin was in court listening as the city demanded $15,000 in damages for the boycott and insisted that the car pool be discontinued. During a recess from the trial, a reporter ran into the courtroom and handed a press release to Martin.

As he read it, Martin's fear changed to glee: "The

Thousands Boarded the Integrated Buses.

MARTIN LUTHER KING, JR.

United States Supreme Court today affirmed a decision of a special three-judge U.S. District Court in declaring Alabama's state and local laws requiring segregation on buses unconstitutional," the release read.

"God Almighty has spoken from Washington, D.C.," Martin told his friends and supporters.

More than a month later, December 20, the mandate from the Supreme Court arrived in Montgomery. Martin, Ralph Abernathy, Nixon and Glenn Smiley—a white minister and member of the pioneering civil rights group, the Fellowship of Reconciliation—took a ride on the city's first integrated bus.

This symbolic gesture was soon matched by the day-to-day reality as thousands of black and white citizens boarded the integrated buses without any major incident, although the Ku Klux Klan held several demonstrations protesting the new conditions. It was a victory won at great cost: The MIA spent $225,000 in court fees, transportation and other expenses. The bus company lost $250,000 in revenues. Also, the city and local merchants took sizable financial losses during the eleven-month-long strike.

The celebration, however, lost some of its luster with the continued resistance from some white ministers, who were slow to support integration. Some of them did not want to get involved in an issue that would bring them unwanted attention; nor did the White Citizens Council accept the new conditions. There were people who resorted to racist activities in order to stand in the way of the move toward harmony. Despite these setbacks, in a few days the city began to experience a period of peace.

And just when Martin and Reverend Abernathy

Protesting the New Conditions

thought they could take a break from the intense struggle, word came that Abernathy's house and church had been bombed. When they arrived at Abernathy's house, the street was roped off and a crowd stood staring at the ruins.

The front porch was completely destroyed. Inside, things were scattered from one room to the next. Several more black churches were also ripped by bombs. Damages from the bombings of these churches was estimated at $7,000.

In response to the disasters, the city commission ordered all buses removed from the streets. Martin worried that the spread of violence might cancel the bus company's license.

Shortly after the bombing of Abernathy's home and church, Dr. King participated in joining with sixty other leading ministers in the founding of the Southern Christian Leadership Conference. As usual, Martin was elected to head the new organization.

These leaders worked hard for peace, but the bombings continued, rocking the city with fear. Faced with a growing emergency, the city was compelled to act. Rewards were offered to help bring about the arrest and conviction of those responsible for the lawlessness. Many were suprised when seven white men were arrested, and five of them were brought before a grand jury.

Based on their own experience, many black residents did not believe the men would be convicted. Unfortunately, they were right. Despite a mountain of evidence, including signed confessions, the men were found not guilty. Such was often the case in the South at that time.

But the Montgomery boycott was not a lost cause. It had introduced America to a new voice that would

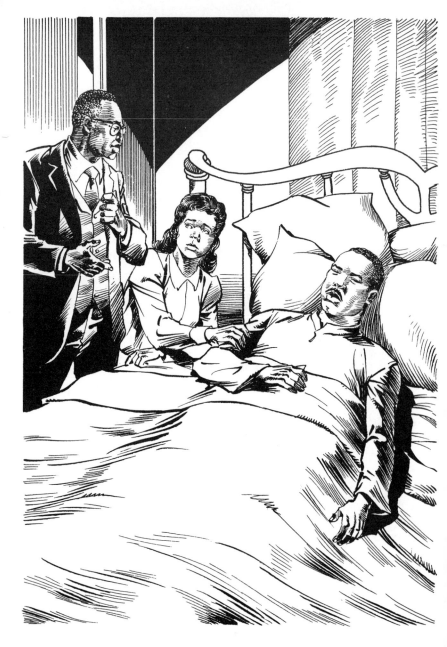

Sheer Exhaustion

speak eloquently, on behalf of the poor and the oppressed, for the next thirteen years. And even at this early stage of Martin Luther King, Jr.'s career, the burden of leadership was a heavy one. At age twenty-eight, Dr. King collapsed from sheer exhaustion. He needed rest—but he wasn't going to get it for long.

The civil rights movement had begun.

Chapter 4

In the National Spotlight

Fame came almost immediately. Martin and Coretta were invited in March, 1957 to join a delegation of noted men and women on a journey to Africa to witness the independence of the new nation of Ghana. Traveling with some of the leading black American figures of the time— Ralph Bunche, Adam Clayton Powell and A. Philip Randolph—was a special experience for Martin, but he was already gaining the attention of some of the most outstanding ministers in the South. The name Martin Luther

Leading Figures of the Time

MARTIN LUTHER KING, JR.

King, Jr., was beginning to be widely recognized.

On their return from Africa, the Kings stopped in Rome, Italy; Geneva, Switzerland; London and Paris. Arriving in New York City, they met with black leaders who were planning a proposal for a large gathering in Washington, D.C.

That May, more than 35,000 people gathered in the nation's capital for a Prayer Pilgrimage for Freedom. A number of speakers, including Dr. King, stressed the need to encourage all black Americans to register to vote, the Constitutional right of all Americans. These marchers set the stage for the historic March on Washington D.C. six years later, in 1963.

No sooner had Martin taken a major step forward onto the world stage, than he was forced to take one step back—to jail. Martin and Coretta were at Recorder's Court in Montgomery accompanying the

Reverend Abernathy and his wife, Juanita, one day in September, when Martin was accosted by two police officers who claimed he had acted improperly.

The police grabbed Martin, pinning his arms behind his back. Then, they hustled him around to the jailhouse, and flung him into a cell.

Coretta tried to come to his aid, but Martin pleaded with her to stay out of the way. Locked inside the jail cell, Martin thought about the lessons that nonviolence teaches, and the importance of enduring hardships, sometimes, for one's beliefs. This was the philosophy of India's famous religious leader, Mahatma Gandhi, whom Martin deeply admired. Gandhi had led his people to political independence from a harsh government. Martin wanted to try to lead his people to freedom as well—to be like the Mahatma, which means "man of wisdom."

Every racial incident now made Martin more

Assaulted by a Crazed Woman

famous and more popular among black Americans, who were starved for heroes of their own. Such popularity, however, was not without danger. In September, 1958, during a promotional tour for his first book, *Stride Toward Freedom,* Dr. King was assaulted by a crazed woman. He was signing books at Blumstein's, a department store in Harlem, when an elderly black woman approached him.

"Are you Mr. King?" she asked.

"Yes, I am," Martin answered.

"Luther King, I been after you for five years," she exclaimed, pulling a steel letter opener from beneath her dress. She had mistaken Martin for someone else.

But before he could say another word, the woman began stabbing Martin with the letter opener and beating him with her fist. Martin fell back into a nearby chair, stunned by the attack. The police arrived and took the woman away. Martin was rushed to Harlem Hospital with the weapon protruding from his chest.

To remove the letter opener, the surgeons had to break one of Martin's ribs, which left him with a permanent scar in the shape of a cross. Because the tip of the blade had touched his aorta—the heart's main artery—the operation was a delicate one.

Four days later, Martin was moving about the hospital in a wheelchair, receiving visitors and reading hundreds of sympathy letters.

One letter in particular was very heartwarming: "What makes you think you are the 'exclusive property' of the Negro race only?" a white woman wrote. "You belong to us too, because we love you. Your voice is the only true voice of love today.... Please don't lose faith in us 'whites,' there are so many of us who are good and pray for your triumph."

The Operation Was a Delicate One.

MARTIN LUTHER KING, JR.

While recovering from the stabbing, Martin thought seriously about accepting an invitation to visit India, the birthplace of Mahatma Gandhi, whom he admired so much. In the first week of February, 1959, Dr. King and his wife left for a journey across India, a trip that would last four weeks. The Kings met with many Indian leaders, including an official dinner with Prime Minister Jawaharlal Nehru.

Martin was saddened by the thousands of poor people he saw in India, but he was excited to visit the sites where Mahatma Gandhi had led his non-violent war of independence.

And there was something else that Martin saw in India that inspired him. He was deeply impressed by the way the Indian government was trying to help their disadvantaged people.

In India, society is divided into groups, an

arrangement called the caste system. In the caste system, a person born into a lower caste, or a poorer group, must spend his or her entire life as a member of that caste. A person born into a higher caste—someone born into a wealthy family, for instance—will remain in that caste, too.

People born into the very lowest caste of all are called "untouchables," and it was always traditionally impossible, in India, for untouchables to have the opportunity to better themselves.

Prime Minister Nehru explained to Martin that India now had a new program to help untouchables. If an untouchable and someone from a higher caste were trying to get into the same college, the untouchable would be given the first chance. This way, Nehru explained, the government was trying to end so much discrimination toward members of the lower castes.

The Kings Flew to Jerusalem.

MARTIN LUTHER KING, JR.

Martin knew then that this was the kind of change he wanted to bring to his own country. He promised himself he would never stop trying.

From the roads that Gandhi traveled, the Kings flew to Jerusalem, Israel to retrace for themselves some of the paths that Jesus walked.

Then it was on to Cairo, Egypt and Athens, Greece where they viewed the ancient landmarks they had only read about in books before.

As soon as Martin was back home, he set about further study of the principles of nonviolent protest which had such a deep effect on him.

Martin also had to make a decision about whether he was going to remain in Montgomery, or go back to Atlanta where his father needed a co-pastor. On November 30, 1959, Martin made the announcement that he was returning to Atlanta and his father's church.

"The time has come," he said, "for a bold, broad advance of the Southern campaign for equality.... We must not let the strategic opportunity pass. Very soon our new program will be announced. Not only will it include a stepped-up campaign of voter registration, but a full-scale assault will be made upon discrimination and segregation in all forms. We must train our youth and adult leaders in the techniques of social change through nonviolent resistance.

"We must employ new methods of struggle involving the masses of the people."

Another reason for moving back to Atlanta was to be closer to the Southern Christian Leadership Conference (SCLC) and its operations.

Student sit-ins had started. Young black protesters, along with white equal-rights supporters, would enter areas that were for whites only and refuse to

Student Sit-Ins Had Started.

leave, risking arrest and jail. Martin's father and other older leaders were opposed to the sit-ins. They believed the best way to secure civil rights for all was through the courts and voting booths.

But Martin Luther King, Jr., felt differently. He praised the students' zeal and their nonviolent behavior. Soon he joined them, and was arrested for sitting in the Magnolia Room restaurant of Rich's Department store in Atlanta.

Martin may have forgotten he had been arrested earlier for driving without a license—but the police didn't. While he watched others being released, Martin was held for violating probation. He was sent to Reidsville State Penitentiary to serve a four-month sentence.

After spending eight days in prison, Dr. King was released on a $2,000 bond. Later, it was disclosed that Senator John F. Kennedy's brother Robert

Kennedy, who was then Senator Kennedy's presidential campaign manager, had made a call to the judge asking that Dr. King be freed.

In March, 1961, after several speaking engagements and TV shows, Martin returned to Atlanta to find the city on the edge of a riot. Although an agreement for change had been reached between the Chamber of Commerce and a group of black leaders including Martin's father, the city's younger, more militant blacks were dissatisfied with the settlement. They accused their elders of selling them out.

An open meeting was called at a local church to debate the issue. Martin's father attempted to keep the crowd orderly, but was hooted from the pulpit. Martin Jr., stepped up and calmly explained the settlement.

"This contract," he began, "is the first one ever written by the white leaders of Atlanta." His speech

White Members Sat in the Back of the Bus.

had a cooling effect on the audience. The majority of people at the meeting decided to give the city a chance to live up to its promises. Not long afterwards, the students ended their sit-ins, the Atlanta schools were desegregated and the lunch counters at the hotels were opened to black patrons.

The gains made in Atlanta did not spread easily to other parts of the South. Other methods of protest were needed to end the old racial restrictions. The idea of Freedom Rides was created by the Congress of Racial Equality (CORE) and its courageous leader, James Farmer. They intended to fight segregation in transportation.

CORE's aim was to test the Supreme Court decision that had outlawed segregated seating on interstate buses and trains. To make their point, white members of CORE would sit in the back of the bus and blacks would sit in the front, and they would all refuse to move when ordered.

At every rest stop, blacks would attempt to use all the rest rooms marked whites-only. When the riders, all of them carefully chosen, arrived in Atlanta, they met with Dr. King and his staff at the Southern Christian Leadership Conference. Martin decided to provide these courageous protesters with financial support for their trip to Alabama.

The reception for the Freedom Riders in Anniston and Birmingham was rough and violent. At the Anniston bus depot, a gang of whites hurled stones at the bus. Later, when the bus stopped to repair a tire, the mob returned and someone tossed a firebomb through the rear door. The bus was an inferno of raging fire as passengers fled for safety.

As the second bus arrived in Birmingham, it too was greeted by a mob of angry whites. The riders were viciously assaulted. Unfortunately, one white

The Reception Was Rough and Violent.

man, William Barbee, was permanently paralyzed in the violent attack. The police commissioner, Bull Connor, and the governor were not sympathetic to a group they said were "lawbreakers."

The courage of the CORE riders sparked the nation. A group of students from Nashville assembled in Birmingham, promising to journey to Montgomery. Their fate was no different. They were set upon by thousands of racists who clubbed them with pipes and baseball bats. Along with the rest of the nation, Dr. King sorrowfully watched the beatings and heard the name-calling on television.

"Ralph," Martin told his friend, the Reverend Abernathy over the phone, "I can't take any more of this. I'm on my way there."

Robert Kennedy, who was now the Attorney General, begged him not to, since he could not guarantee Martin's safety.

MARTIN LUTHER KING, JR.

A mass rally was called that evening at the Reverend Abernathy's church. The church was soon surrounded by an angry mob. Heckling and shouting, the mob began throwing stones and tear-gas containers through the windows. Martin hurried to the basement and placed a call to the Attorney General. Kennedy promised him that Federal marshals were on their way.

Suddenly, the mob outside was quiet. It was an eerie silence. Martin peered through a window to see what was happening. He was happy to see that the marshals had arrived and were forcing the crowd to leave. Now Martin's followers inside could go home in peace and quiet.

Things were not so peaceful, though, for the Freedom Riders who were determined to continue their journey to Mississippi—against Martin's better judgment.

Hundreds of Protesters Thrown into Jail

MARTIN LUTHER KING, JR.

In Mississippi the riders were arrested, and this made matters worse. Hundreds of protesters arrived at the scene only to be thrown in jail too. Soon, all across the South, Freedom Riders were boldly daring to defy the law. Dr. King and his aides worked around the clock raising the money to pay their fines, only to see them arrested again.

All over the world, people were aware of the violence and protest in the American South. It was impossible to ignore so many incidents of social unrest. The Federal government had to take action now. Under pressure from the Attorney General's office, the Interstate Commerce Commission issued regulations ending segregated rest rooms in interstate bus stations. The regulations were to be effective November 1, 1961. Once more, with courage and committment, these bold young civil rights workers had accomplished a major goal. But there would still be many difficulties ahead of them.

Caught in the middle of all this social and political activity, Dr. King had very little time for his family, which now included two children—six-year-old Yolanda, "Yoki," and four-year-old Marty. Time with his children was important to Martin and he spent as much time as he could with them, telling them all about his travels and experiences. He played games with them, told them jokes and read them stories. Martin knew how important it is to read together and spend time as a family.

There were also family trips to parks and playgrounds, but Martin was so busy, the basic raising of the children was seen to by Coretta. By 1963, Martin and Coretta had welcomed two more children—Dexter and Bernice.

In addition to his family obligations, Martin's commitment to his church and to his beliefs were in

Time with His Children Was Important.

many ways never-ending. Fortunately, his responsibilities at the SCLC were made easier by the addition of the Reverend Wyatt T. Walker, the executive director, and the presence of Martin's lifelong friend, the Reverend Ralph Abernathy, who had now moved to Atlanta.

Nothing could have pleased Martin more than to have his trusted friend Abernathy nearby. Over the years, they had been as close as two brothers. Martin often said that without the Reverend Abernathy he could have never been able to achieve half of what he did. "I want you to know how much I appreciate your loyalty," Martin told him many times. And Abernathy was devoted to Martin, attending to all the little duties and details that made it easier for Martin to handle the larger, more pressing assignments.

"For Martin," Abernathy would write in his

autobiography, "my coming to Atlanta was an important ingredient in his life, something he had been determined to accomplish, despite my pleas that I didn't want to be 'saved' from Montgomery.

"On the other hand, I can certainly see how much the friendship meant to me since I felt compelled to make the move despite the knowledge that my wife and children would suffer some displacement and my congregation at First Baptist would have to go through the ordeal of finding a new pastor.

"While the scope of my ministry and the future of the civil rights movement played an important part in my decision, finally I think I made the move because Martin wanted me to come to Atlanta so badly."

Now that the two friends were together, they could combine their talents when a crisis arose. Before long, there was indeed a new crisis in the

The Students Refused to Leave.

nation's headlines. Like many parts of the deep South, Albany, Georgia was a stronghold of segregation, and in the summer of 1961, representatives of the Student Nonviolent Coordinating Committee (SNCC) arrived in town to combat racial discrimination.

Their first move was to organize the students and local residents alike. Within a few days a group of students sat down, according to plan, in the whites-only waiting room of the Albany Trailways bus terminal and refused to leave.

The police came and ordered the protesters out. The students obeyed. While they made their point that segregation was still alive in Albany, unfortunately the SNCC activists also angered the city's branch of the National Association for the Advancement of Colored People (NAACP), who disagreed with the students' methods and feared they were trying to lure members away from the NAACP.

If the police ignored the first wave of sit-ins at the bus station, they did not do so at the rallies that followed. Hundreds of protesters were arrested. When Dr. King arrived in Albany and was arrested, he turned down bail money that was raised for him. But he later agreed to be released because he did not want to stand in the way of a settlement. Still, the city leaders failed to integrate the bus terminal or to meet with black leaders.

Dr. King Was Arrested.

Chapter 5

Marching for Freedom

Martin returned once again to Albany, Georgia in February, 1962 to stand trial for his December arrest. Dr. King and Abernathy were sentenced to serve forty-five days in jail or to pay a $78 fine.

"We will serve the time," they said in one voice.

President Kennedy was upset when he heard that Martin was on his way to a prison labor gang on a county road. The President quickly contacted the Justice Department; however, while an assistant attorney general was seeking their release, Martin and Abernathy were freed under mysterious circumstances.

The police chief told Martin that an unidentified black man had paid their fines. They learned later that the chief himself had arranged their release. The move surprised them, and Abernathy commented that he'd been thrown out of lot of places before, "but I've never been thrown out of jail!" By having Martin and Abernathy released, the police chief had prevented them from gaining any publicity from their jail sentences. It was this sort of publicity, though, that was one of the most powerful ways Martin Luther King brought his message to the world.

Toward the end of July, Martin was back behind bars in Albany. This time he spent two weeks in jail for demonstrating. He was released in August. After a series of disappointing discussions, Martin

Martin Lashed Out.

eft Albany, leaving the civil rights work to local
eople.

"When Martin left Albany he was very
epressed," said Andrew Young, who was then a
taff member at the Southern Christian Leadership
Conference. "He knew what had happened." Martin
eared that the civil rights movement in Albany
night have been sabotaged by the Justice Depart-
nent.

Martin was so depressed over this latest defeat in
Albany that he even lashed out at the FBI. "One of
the greatest problems we face with the FBI in the
outh," he told the press, "is that agents are white
outherners who have been influenced by their com-
nunity. To maintain their status, they have to be
riendly with the local police and people who are
romoting segregation. Every time I saw FBI men
n Albany, they were with the local police force."

MARTIN LUTHER KING, JR.

For several months after the Albany setback, Martin had little contact with the public. He seemed to be unhappy, though friends told him that he had made a difference in Albany. At last, he agreed. "Negroes have straightened their backs in Albany," Martin said, "and once a man straightens his back you can't ride him any more."

But there were still white racists in the South who did not want equal rights for African Americans. Dr. King was speaking in Birmingham during an SCLC convention when a white supremacist leaped on stage and struck him.

After the attacker was caught by SCLC members and police, Martin asked that no charges be brought. "This system that we live under creates such people," Martin explained. "I'm not interested in pressing charges. I'm interested in changing the kind of system that produces this kind of man."

A White Supremist Leaped on Stage.

MARTIN LUTHER KING, JR.

Another troubled city on the verge of explosion in the spring of 1963 was Birmingham, Alabama. Martin had spent much of his time since the Albany confrontation traveling around the nation, raising funds for the Southern Christian Leadership Conference. Aware of the courageous struggle against discrimination in Birmingham, Martin focused attention on that city. Members of the SCLC devoted lots of time and study to this next campaign—they did not want to make the same mistakes that had been made in Albany.

Martin and Abernathy went to Birmingham and began holding meetings at various churches, hoping they could gather the people needed to carry out a long struggle. Two small protest marches and sit-ins were not effective. A march to the Federal building was far more successful. Forty-two people were arrested, creating lots of publicity.

MARTIN LUTHER KING, JR.

Then hundreds of protesters took to the streets. This huge gathering was historic, but when public-safety commissioner Eugene "Bull" Connor set loose dogs on the demonstrators, the nation, watching on TV, reacted with horror.

With each day the demonstrations increased as the Birmingham jails were crowded with protesters. The nearby Bessemer jail and the Jefferson County jails were filled to capacity. A few days before Easter Sunday, Dr. King was arrested along with fifty other demonstrators.

Placed in solitary confinement, Martin began to compose his famous "Letter from a Birmingham Jail." Martin addressed his fellow clergymen. Some of them had openly disagreed with his work. In this letter he wrote:

"While confined here in the Birmingham city jail, I came across your recent statement calling my

"Letter from a Birmingham Jail"

activities 'unwise and untimely.' Seldom do I pause to answer criticism of my work and ideas...but since I feel that you are men of genuine good will and your criticisms are sincerely set forth, I would like to answer your statement....

"The purpose of our direct-action program is to create a situation so crisis-packed that it will inevitably open the door to negotiation....Too long has our beloved South-land been bogged down in a tragic effort to live in monologue rather than dialogue...

"We know through painful experience that freedom is never voluntarily given by the oppressor; it must demanded by the oppressed....Frankly, I have yet to engage in a direct-action campaign that was 'well-timed' in view of those who have not suffered unduly from the disease of segregation. For years now I have heard the word 'Wait!' It rings in the ear of every Negro.... This 'Wait' has almost always meant 'Never.' We must come to see ... that 'justice too long delayed is justice denied.' "

Martin's long letter was written mostly on scraps of paper and smuggled out of the jail a few pages at a time.

While Dr. King was in jail, the civil rights movement gathered strength. Day after day large crowds clashed with police who brutalized them. It is said that blood flowed in the streets. But all of these brutal attacks, including vicious dogs and thunderous streams of water sprayed from full-force fire hoses, could not stop the tide of civil resistance.

Martin was in jail for a week before he was released. This pushed the protest up to another level. With their backs agains the wall from the show of unity and strength by Martin and his followers, the city's merchants asked for a temporary

Dogs and Fire Hoses

peace in order to discuss a possible agreement.

An accord was finally announced. It was a tremendous victory for the civil rights movement. Martin's determination to use nonviolent forms of protest was successful. It was also the dramatic beginning to an even more important step.

Martin's victorious campaign in Birmingham did not go unnoticed at the White House. In June, President Kennedy told the nation it was time to grant all Americans equal rights and equal opportunities. "Who among us would be content to have the color of his skin changed and stand in his place?" said Kennedy, speaking on behalf of all black Americans. "Who among us would then be content with the counsels of patience and delay?" What was needed was a civil rights bill, and no one had pushed President Kennedy harder on this matter than his brother, Robert, the Attorney General.

MARTIN LUTHER KING, JR.

The news was cheered in the black community. People greeted the bill like a second Emancipation Proclamation, the great freedom-document issued by President Abraham Lincoln in 1863, freeing the slaves in parts of the South.

But it was the response from racists that caught everybody's attention next. On the very same evening of Kennedy's speech, Medgar Evers, an NAACP leader in Jackson, Mississippi, was murdered on his doorstep. Evers was a fearless man, greatly admired, and a deeply devoted father to his young family.

"He could talk to the children and tell them what was happening," his wife, Myrlie, recalled, "and he devised a game with them where they decided what was the safest place in the house to hide if something happened. The children made a decision with their father that the bathtub was safest. They could

Evers's Death Deeply Troubled Martin.

not understand everything, but they were well aware that their father's life was in danger. At their young ages—three, eight, nine—they worried constantly about that."

News of Evers's death deeply troubled Martin, and he was reminded of the danger he faced as a leader. "Negroes tragically know political assassination well," he wrote in his book *Why We Can't Wait*. "In the life of Negro civil rights leaders, the whine of the bullet from ambush, the roar of the bomb have all too often broken the night's silence."

Besides Evers, there were many others murdered in the civil rights movement during this period, including Mr. and Mrs. Harry T. Moore, NAACP leaders in Florida; the Reverend George Lee of Belzoni, Mississippi; William Moore in Alabama; and most tragically, four little black girls—Carole Robertson, Cynthia Wesley, Denise McNair, and

Addie Mae Collins—who died after the bombing of the 16th Street Baptist Church in Birmingham, Alabama, less than a month after the historic March on Washington.

"The thundering events of the summer required an appropriate climax," Martin said. "The dean of Negro leaders, A. Philip Randolph...once again provided the uniquely suitable answer. He proposed a March on Washington to unite, in one luminous action, all of the forces along the far-flung front."

A March on Washington

Chapter 6

I Have A Dream!

The day of the March was sunny and bright. There was a feeling of unity and victory in the air as 250,000 people gathered along the mall stretching from the Lincoln Memorial to the Washington Monument. Among the marchers waiting to hear a list of well-known speakers were some 60,000 white people, many of them representing labor unions. Stationed on the edge of the grounds were squadrons of police and more than 4,000 military troops. They were prepared for violence—but it never came.

What did come were some of the most memorable words in American history. Martin Luther King cast a spell over listeners with his historic "I Have a Dream" speech.

"I have a dream that one day this nation will rise up and live out the true meaning of its creed: 'We hold these truths to be self-evident; that all men are created equal,'" Martin began, at first reading from a text and then speaking from his heart. "I have a dream that one day on the red hills of Georgia the sons of former slaves and the sons of former slave-owners will be able to sit down together at the table of brotherhood."

With each stage of the speech, Martin was hailed with loud cheering and applause. And an outbreak like thunder rose with his closing remarks: "Let freedom ring from every hill and molehill of Mississippi.

"Free At Last!"

MARTIN LUTHER KING, JR.

From every mountainside, let freedom ring. When we let freedom ring, when we let it ring from every village and hamlet, from every state and every city, we will be able to speed up that day when all of God's children, black men and white men, Jews and Gentiles, Protestants and Catholics, will be able to join hands and sing in the words of the old Negro spiritual: 'Free at last! Free at last! Thank God Almighty, we are free at last!'"

But a terrible sense of loss soon replaced all the happiness and hope Dr. King and others had brought to both black and white Americans with the march.

Martin was at home in Atlanta packing for yet another trip when he heard that President John Fitzgerald Kennedy had been assassinated. Stunned by the news, Martin stopped and sat silently in front of the TV with his wife and a close friend.

"I don't think I'm going to live to be forty," Martin said to Coretta.

"Don't say that, Martin," she replied.

"This is going to happen to me also," Martin said, and then fell silent.

Martin was hurt by the loss of a president he was just getting to know. Now it would be necessary to start all over again, to try to convey his ideas to the new President, Lyndon Johnson, who had nearly always voted against civil rights legislation when he had served in the Senate.

But Martin had more to worry about. Weary after a year filled with more than 300 speeches and nearly 280,000 miles of travel across the nation, Martin saw problems right in his own hometown where the progress of desegregation effort had virtually come to a halt.

"Don't Say That, Martin."

MARTIN LUTHER KING, JR.

The summer of 1964 was one of discontent and riots. In the Northern black communities of Newark, Philadelphia, Chicago and Harlem, citizens turned to violence, burning and looting until curfews were ordered. President Johnson called a meeting with Dr. King and other black leaders.

Martin went to Harlem, but was forced to leave after being called an "outsider" and threatened by local residents. Martin turned once more to hate-filled Mississippi to observe the Freedom Summer campaign to educate and register black people to vote.

Traveling through the rural counties of Mississippi—"the state that has four eyes but cannot see"—was very dangerous. There were several threats on Martin's life.

And nowhere was the threat of trouble as great as it was in Philadelphia, Mississippi. A search was on to find three missing civil rights workers. In August, the bad news came that the bodies of the three young men—James Chaney, Michael Schwerner, and Andrew Goodman—one black and the others white, had been found in an earthen dam near Philadelphia. The names of three more courageous young men were added to the growing list of people who had given their lives for the civil rights movement. The Freedom Summer campaign was stained with the sorrow of the loss of many dedicated volunteers.

Martin was back on the political trail, trying to get the Democratic Party to discuss the problems of the nation's poor and needy at the Democratic National Convention. Martin's next effort was on behalf of the mostly black delegates from the Mississippi Freedom Democratic Party. His task was to get them seated at the Convention. His effort was

He Had Won the Nobel Peace Prize.

partly successful, and even some success meant a lot.

Overworked from a busy schedule that included the many speeches he gave opposing the candidacy of Senator Barry Goldwater, Martin took a break from his usual nonstop routine. Then came the amazing news that he had won the Nobel Peace Prize.

Martin and Coretta were moved and delighted. Amid the excitement, he told the press that most of the prize money—$54,600—would be donated to various civil rights organizations, including his own Southern Christian Leadership Conference, and to the Student Nonviolent Coordinating Committee. Now Martin had an honor received by only two other black men—Ralph Bunche and South African patriot Albert Lutuli. Most Americans were thrilled and proud that Martin Luther King received the award.

On receiving the prize, Martin said, "I refuse to accept the view that mankind is so tragically bound to the starless midnight of racism and war that the bright daylight of peace and brotherhood can never become a reality. I believe that even amid today's mortar bursts and whining bullets, there is still hope for a brighter tomorrow."

Eight days later there was a reception for Dr. King at the White House, where he told President Johnson that his plan for a voting rights bill would be a good follow-up to the Civil Rights Act that Congress had passed earlier. But nothing was ever guaranteed in the struggle for civil rights—the conflict of Selma, Alabama was next.

While SNCC workers had been fighting against segregation in this Alabama city for several months, it was not until the passage of the Civil Rights Act

A Reception at the White House

that they felt strong enough to become more daring in their demands.

The marches began on January 18. Martin led them first to a restaurant and then to the courthouse. No one was arrested because the sheriff ordered the demonstrators to assemble in an alley behind the courthouse. The city's white leaders were determined not to do anything to attract the media. They thought that they could keep the disturbances under control, there would be nothing to report, and the press would soon go away. That plan lasted one day, until pictures of the sheriff himself beating a protester appeared in major newspapers across the nation. The whole world could see what was happening in Selma.

As the conflict and beatings increased, Martin, the Nobel Peace Prize winner, and 250 marchers were arrested and taken to the city jail. His picture was on the front pages of newspapers everywhere. All across America, people could see the man the whole world had recently honored being treated like a common criminal. From jail, Martin sent telegrams to important political leaders, including congressmen.

In Washington, President Johnson was alarmed by the events in Selma and made the issue of voting rights a top priority. Many black people felt that a voting rights act was long overdue. There was a flurry of activity between Washington and Selma, including a quickly arranged meeting between Dr. King and the President.

Still, the city was in turmoil and the death toll was rising. Jimmie Lee Jackson, a young black man, was killed when he fought back after a police officer had struck his mother.

Coretta sadly recalled that Jackson's aunt was

"Why Must Good Men Die . . ."

one of her best friends in high school. Several weeks after delivering the eulogy at Jackson's funeral, Martin regretted having yet another one to perform. This time the victim was white—James Reeb, a Unitarian minister from Boston. Reeb was killed by four members of a large organization of violent white racists, the KKK—Ku Klux Klan.

"Why must good men die for good?" Martin asked in the eulogy at Reeb's funeral, which was held in Selma and attended by 2,000 people. Never in the nation's history had so many people from different religious faiths attended a funeral.

"James Reeb's death may cause the white South to come to terms with its conscience," Martin continued. The thousands at the memorial service were not the only Americans moved by the senseless crime in Selma.

President Johnson said, "What happened in

MARTIN LUTHER KING, JR.

Selma is part of a far larger movement which reaches into every section and state of America. It is the effort of American Negroes to secure for themselves the full blessings of American life." Johnson promised that the Voting Rights Bill would be among the top items on his agenda.

A fifty-mile-march was proposed to go from Selma to the Alabama state capital, the city of Montgomery. To make the trip meant the marchers would have to cross a bridge along a well-traveled highway. George Wallace, the then governor of Alabama and a fierce opponent of the civil rights movement, vowed not to permit the march because it would tie up highway traffic.

It would be a very dangerous trip. Some SNCC leaders opposed it. Even so, when the decision was made, Hosea Williams, a leader of the SCLC, and SNCC leader John Lewis, were out front, marching

From Selma to Montgomery

side by side.

"When we arrived at the apex of the Edmund Pettus Bridge," Lewis recalled, "we saw a sea of . . . Alabama state troopers." The officer in charge of the troopers warned the marchers that they were breaking the law. But the marchers ignored the officer, and the state troopers advanced against the marchers, swinging the billy clubs. Tear gas was released and the marchers scrambled for cover, gasping for breath.

Martin watched news accounts of the attack, which reporters began to call Bloody Sunday, from Atlanta. He then sent telegrams to a number of top clergymen, asking them to join him in Selma. On the appointed day and hour, despite pleas from the president and other important officials, Martin led 1,500 people out of the church and across Pettus Bridge. The Alabama state troopers were waiting.

MARTIN LUTHER KING, JR.

Martin asked the Reverend Abernathy to lead the marchers in prayer. But suddenly he decided to halt the march. "I didn't want to see anyone harmed," Martin explained later. It was a low point for the marchers, though their spirits were soon lifted.

President Johnson announced the voting rights legislation before Congress. It was following this that Johnson delivered a famous speech which included the moving words of a Negro spiritual—the song that had become a slogan of the civil rights movement—"We Shall Overcome." That the President of the United States had included himself by saying the word "we" sent a message to the entire country that we are one people, a nation of many different colors.

Not long after this historic moment, a judge ruled that the marchers were within their constitutional rights to go from Selma to Montgomery.

Full of Hope

Chapter 7

Old and New Struggles
for Justice

On March 21, some four thousand people gathered behind Dr. King, Ralph Bunche and Rabbi
Abraham Joshua Heschel, of the Jewish Theological
Seminary, for the long march to Montgomery. The
marchers started their journey full of hope.

All different kinds of people participated in this
march for freedom, many carrying large U.S. flags.
There were nuns, farmers, teenagers, news
reporters—even a one-legged white man on

crutches—as the huge crowd of demonstrators marched slowly down Jefferson Davis Highway.

Near the end of the five-day march, this caravan of people had grown to 25,000. Rumors spread that when they reached Montgomery, Martin would be assassinated. But Martin marched on. And since he had no intention of leaving the marchers, something had to be done to protect him.

"Martin always wore the good-preacher blue suit," Andrew Young recalled later. "And I figured since we couldn't stop him from marching, everybody who was about Martin's size and had a blue suit, I put in front of the line." Young said that none of those men in blue suits were aware of what was going on at the time.

At last, the marches reached Montgomery. Martin walked the final few feet up the steps to the capitol building and addressed the crowd: "However

25,000 People

difficult the moment, however frustrating the hour, it will not be long, because truth crushed to the earth will rise again. How long? Not long. Because you shall reap what you sow. How long? Not long... because the arc of the moral universe is long, but it bends towards justice. How long? Not long. Because mine eyes have seen the glory of the coming of the Lord."

Martin wanted to call on Governor Wallace, to present him a petition asking him to remove the discriminatory regulations that kept blacks from registering to vote.

"The governor is not in," Martin was informed, so the petition was given to the governor's executive secretary. After the petition was delivered, the marchers decided that it would be best to get out of Montgomery as fast as possible, since there had been threats of danger.

MARTIN LUTHER KING, JR.

Among the number of car owners who had volunteered to drive some of the marchers back to Selma was Viola Liuzzo, a white homemaker from Detroit. She completed one trip to Selma and then returned to Montgomery. A young black man rode with her.

As they drove down Route 80, a car with four Ku Klux Klansmen in it pulled alongside them. Shots were fired, and two of the bullets hit Mrs. Liuzzo, killing her as her car veered off into a ditch. The young black man riding with Mrs. Liuzzo, aware that the murderers were peering into the car, pretended to be dead. Blood on his clothing helped him to create the illusion. When the men left, he got out of the car and flagged down a passing motorist, who happened to be another demonstrator. Later it was reported that one of the four men in the car, Gary Rowe, was an FBI informant.

"As a mother," wrote Coretta King, "I felt my

The President Signed the Voting Rights Bill.

heart go out to her now motherless children, and to her devoted husband who had been widowed and now had the sole responsibility for the children. Of course, what had obviously inflamed the racists who killed her had been the sight of a white woman in a car with black man, on a dark Alabama road."

There had been a mountain of obstacles, and many had given their lives, but nothing could stop the joy that was heard when President Johnson signed the Voting Rights Bill on August 6, 1965.

Segregation by law, which existed all over the South, was dealt a crippling blow. Beyond the law, though, segregation was still practiced both in the North and in the South. Martin wanted to carry the idea of nonviolent protest to the North. He went to Chicago to lead a big demonstration in the summer of 1965.

When Martin got to Chicago, he joined his aides,

but rather than taking a room at a hotel, he and Coretta chose to move into slum housing in a poverty-stricken section of the city. They wanted to show their support to their followers who were poor.

Coretta recalled: "It was a railroad flat, with a sitting room in front and the rest of the rooms going straight back—two bedrooms, a kitchen, and a bath of sorts. You had to go through the bedrooms to get to the kitchen."

The difference Martin Luther King made to a troubled world can be seen in the work he did while living among the poor. In Chicago Martin made a point of working with the street gangs. "We held workshops with the gang leaders, trying to communicate the discipline of nonviolence," Coretta wrote in her memoir. "In the end, many members of the gangs pledged themselves to nonviolence, and demonstrated with us in accordance with our

They Moved into Slum Housing.

beliefs. The effectiveness of our work with the Chicago teenage gangs is one of the greatest tributes to the nonviolent method, and to my husband's leadership."

The big rally they had planned in Chicago took place on Sunday, July 10, 1966 and was attended by 50,000 people. "I want every black person in Chicago to withdraw their money from the banks and savings and loans companies that practice discrimination," Martin said, "and I want you to boycott those companies that refuse to hire you." Then he led them on a march to City Hall to see the mayor. But City Hall was closed when the marchers arrived.

The next day the mayor agreed to meet with Martin, but nothing came of it. That evening, violence broke out in several sections of Chicago. Martin and Coretta rushed to see if they could do something about the angry rioting.

Although there was a day or two of calm, the disorder soon spread all over the city. Rioters hurled stones through store windows. They rushed in and stole whatever goods they could carry, a crime called looting. "The rioting went on all night," Coretta recalled. "I remember after getting the three younger children to bed, Yolanda and I were looking out the back window at a grocery store a few yards away. Young rioters were looting the store. I heard them when they smashed the glass, and I could see them getting the groceries, piling them into shopping carts, and wheeling them away. It was very distressing to me to watch."

Soon after the rioting ended, Coretta and the children returned to Atlanta. Martin learned that anger and hatred were not just something that happened in the South. Nevertheless, he continued to travel

Operation Breadbasket

back and forth between Atlanta and Chicago, set on keeping the civil rights movement alive.

To fight the growing poverty and joblessness in Chicago, the Southern Christian Leadership Conference formed a relief effort called Operation Breadbasket. This new organization had had some success in Atlanta and in several other southern cities.

A young preacher named Jesse Jackson was given the responsibility of heading the organization. Though it had some impact in helping blacks gain employment, and assisting others to find relief, Operation Breadbasket could not come close to solving the overall problem of poverty, which was so widespread in many black communities of Chicago as in so many other parts of America.

By the spring of 1967, Dr. King was becoming more and more concerned about the war the United States was involved in overseas in Vietnam, a small nation in southeast Asia. More than anything, Martin was angry about the enormous amount of money being spent to support the conflict in Vietnam. "This money," he told friends, "is sorely needed to help feed America's starving masses." According to Martin's estimation, the government spent $322,000 for each enemy soldier killed in Vietnam, but only $35 for each poor person in this country.

Martin prayed for a long while, and later discussed the matter with his family and friends before deciding to speak out against the war in southeast Asia.

Martin chose Riverside Church in New York City as the site where he would speak out to oppose the war in Vietnam, relating it to the civil rights movement.

Martin began in almost a whisper. But then he went on in his strong, stirring voice to deliver this

Martin Prayed for a Long Time.

now historic speech:

"I come to this magnificent house of worship tonight, because my conscience leaves me no other choice. I join with you in this meeting because I am in deepest agreement with the aims and work of the organization which has brought us together: Clergy and Laymen Concerned about Vietnam.

"Over the past two years, as I have moved to break the betrayal of my own silences and to speak from the burnings of my own heart, as I have called for radical departures from the destruction of Vietnam, many persons have questioned me about the wisdom of my path.

"At the heart of their concerns this query has often loomed large and loud: Why are you speaking about war, Dr. King? Why are you joining the voices of dissent? Peace and civil rights don't mix, they say. Aren't you hurting the cause of your people, they may ask?

"And when I hear them, though I often understand the source of their concern, I am nevertheless greatly saddened, for such questions mean that the inquirers have not really known me, my commitment or my calling.

"I come to this platform tonight to make a passionate plea to my beloved nation. A few years ago there was a shining moment in that civil rights struggle. It seemed as if there was a real promise of hope for the poor—both black and white—through the poverty program. There were experiments, hopes, new beginnings.

"Then came the buildup in Vietnam, and I knew America would never invest the necessary funds or energies in rehabilitation of its poor so long as adventures like Vietnam continued to draw men and skills and money like some demonic destructive

"An Enemy of the Poor"

suction tube. So I was increasingly compelled to see the war as an enemy of the poor and to attack it as such."

Martin suggested five concrete things that the government should do immediately to end its involvement in the war:

1. End all bombing in North and South Vietnam.

2. Declare a unilateral cease-fire in the hope that such action will create the atmosphere for negotiation.

3. Take immediate steps to prevent other battlegrounds in Southeast Asia by curtailing our military buildup in Thailand and our interference in Laos.

4. Realistically accept the fact that the National Liberation Front has substantial support in South Vietnam and must thereby play a role in any meaningful negotiations and in any future Vietnamese

government.

5. Set a date that will remove all foreign troops from Vietnam in accordance with the 1954 Geneva Agreement.

Having presented his demands, Martin moved to the close of his long, thoughtful speech, his voice gaining power and persuasion. "We must move past indecision to action," he said. "We must find new ways to speak for peace in Vietnam and justice throughout the developing world—a world that borders on our doors. If we do not act we shall surely be dragged down the long dark and shameful corridors of time reserved for those who possess power without compassion, might without morality, and strength without sight."

From this bold stand Martin became even more outspoken. He spoke of the United States as the

Martin Became Even More Outspoken.

"greatest purveyor of violence today" and remarked, "If America's soul becomes totally poisoned, part of the autopsy must read Vietnam."

Now Dr. King was standing directly in the international spotlight, and he was under surveillance by the Federal Bureau of Investigation (FBI). After this speech, Martin was listed as a "revolutionary" by the FBI. The Johnson administration was concerned too. They were eager to know if Martin's "radical" position against the war might also mean that he was interested in running for political office. Rumors were heard that Martin might run as an anti-war candidate for the presidency in 1968.

There were many ordinary citizens who let Martin know they disliked his position on the war in Vietnam—many people backed the United States' involvement there. They accused Martin with words like "treason" and "communist sympathizer." *New*

York Times editorials said that Martin was wrong to connect the war in Vietnam with the civil rights movement—that the two things were "distinct and separate." Certain black leaders said Martin was wrong for meddling in the government's international policies. There were well-known black Americans, such as Whitney Young, Roy Wilkins and Jackie Robinson, who also criticized Martin's actions at the time.

For a while Martin was hurt by all of these replies, especially the responses from his colleagues.

"I don't understand it," Martin told Coretta at home after his speech in New York was over. "We need to stick together. Solidarity is the key to bringing about real change. *One* voice is what we need, to really be heard!"

"I know," Coretta answered. "But we still have to stand up for our beliefs, even if other black leaders

"He Sees War as an Evil."

disagree with you. Anyone who doesn't agree with you about the war in Vietnam just doesn't understand Martin Luther King—and what Martin Luther King stands for."

In spite of much public criticism of his ideas, Martin held his ground. So did Coretta.

"You cannot believe in peace at home and not believe in international peace," Coretta stated publicly in defense of her husband's philosophy. "He could not be a true follower of the nonviolent philosophy and condone war. You think of him as a politician, but he feels that as a minister he has a prophetic role and must speak out against the evils of society. He sees war as an evil, and therefore he must condemn war."

And speak out he did. "I've fought too long and too hard now against segregated accommodations to end up segregating my moral concerns," he exclaimed. But I know that justice is indivisible. Injustice anywhere is a threat to justice everywhere."

While some of his fellow ministers and so-called friends criticized Martin, others agreed with him. Stokely Carmichael, a new young black spokesman whose angrier, more militant demands for "Black Power" were just starting to receive attention, supported Martin's position. Soon the phrase Black Power was an important part of the vocabulary of the late 1960s. More established black leaders—Bayard Rustin, Floyd McKissick and Benjamin Mays—also supported Dr. King's anti-war view.

As spring turned into summer Martin was still under fire for his position against the war, but now major riots had damaged several big cities and he centered his attention once again on violence here at home.

Riots Damaged Several Big Cities.

"I condemn the violence of riots," he told the press, "but I understand the conditions that cause them. I think we must be just as concerned about correcting those conditions as we are about punishing the guilty." One of the largest riots erupted in Detroit. When the four days of turmoil ended, forty-three lives had been lost and there was more than $50 million in property damage. Martin saw Detroit as a symbol of black people's inner torment and rage.

Some people's rage was encouraged by the speeches being made by Stokely Carmichael, H. Rap Brown and the increasing boldness of a new political group, the Black Panther Party. These young men and women saw themselves as the "children" of Malcolm X, an outspoken black Muslim leader, who believed in ending racism and injustice "by any means necessary."

MARTIN LUTHER KING, JR.

For these new young militants, violence was viewed as sometimes the best way to deal with oppression. It was a time when many young political activists—black and white—were convinced that a revolution was just around the corner. Sadly, they discovered that the only thing around the corner was more death and destruction.

A blazing summer of unrest made Martin think more than ever about the condition of the poor. The plight of those without homes, without health care and without jobs, stayed on his mind, night and day.

"If we can't get government to recognize this part of our population," Martin said to Coretta at the time, "then we're going to have to teach poor people how to get together and speak loudly—shout if they have to—to be heard once and for all."

"You always say that there's strength in numbers," Coretta answered him. "Maybe it's time to

"All People Who Deserve a Better Life"

organize another demonstration."

"Yes. And it's going to be a big one," Martin agreed. "We should call people from all our poverty-stricken areas—from everywhere in the country. People not only from the South—from the North, too. People who have no jobs. People who have no resources."

"But where would all this take place?" Coretta asked.

"We ought to get them marching right into Washington, D.C., Coretta," Martin said. "I think it would really highlight this entire issue. The government can't possibly fail to see so many people gathered all at once to be heard. Not just black people. All people who deserve a better life. American Indians. Puerto Ricans. Mexicans. Poor whites. It would truly be a Poor People's Campaign, Coretta."

But how would such a major action as this be

financed? One answer, Martin believed, was to begin a national speaking tour, which he did in the fall of 1967. The tour was a few weeks old when it had to be interrupted—Martin had to serve a five-day jail sentence in Birmingham. Back in the summer the Supreme Court had voted to uphold a conviction in which Martin and others were found guilty of breaking the law with their demonstrations.

This was Dr. King's nineteenth time behind bars, and it could not have come at a worse time. Disappointed by the setbacks in the civil rights movement, other black leaders disagreeing with him, and harassed by the FBI, Martin experienced a bout of depression; he needed a victory of some sort to wash away the gloomy outlook. Upon release from jail, he started his speaking tour with vigor.

Back Behind Bars

Chapter 8

Poor People's Campaign

On December 4, among friends and worshipers of Ebenezer Church, Martin delivered his first public plan for the Poor People's Campaign. Martin had the congregation electrified and the "Amens" filled the church when he preached about how important it would be to take their cause to Washington, D.C. "America is at a crossroads of history," Martin declared, "and it is critically important for us, as a nation and a society, to choose a new path and move upon it with resolution and courage."

178

MARTIN LUTHER KING, JR.

Martin's plan for a Poor People's Campaign caused the FBI to be concerned about the potential disorder the campaign could cause in the cities. J. Edgar Hoover, the director of the FBI and a man opposed to Dr. King's work, increased surveillance of Martin and the Southern Christian Leadership Conference.

The FBI even assigned a special agent to monitor the leaders of the Poor People's Campaign, hoping to halt its development. It was through the FBI that President Johnson, who was very concerned about a large demonstration taking place in Washington D.C., kept up with the moves and timetable of Martin and his staff.

Johnson was unable to convince Dr. King to call off his march. He warned Martin that he would not tolerate disruption in Washington. But, like the old Negro spiritual he often invoked, Martin was not

"Martin Accepted the Danger."

about to let anything "turn him around."

This doesn't mean that Martin didn't worry about the danger he knew might be waiting for him. He often told Coretta that he probably would not live a long life. "He was not gloomy about his fate," Coretta said. "Martin accepted the danger as a matter of course and it had little effect on his spirits. He was worried about the direction of the movement and about the rise of violence, but, as a person, he was exuberant and full of spirit."

On February 4, 1968 Martin Luther King addressed his congregation at Ebenezer Baptist Church with words that seemed to predict his own fate: "If any of you are around when I have to meet my day, I don't want a long funeral. And if you get somebody to deliver my eulogy, tell them not to talk too long. Tell them not to mention that I have a Nobel Peace Prize. That isn't important.

MARTIN LUTHER KING, JR.

"Tell them not to mention that I have three or four hundred other awards. That's not important. Tell them not to mention where I went to school. I'd like somebody to mention that day, that Martin Luther King, Jr., tried to give his life serving others . . . tried to love somebody."

There was much to do, and many things to pull together if the Poor People's Campaign was going to have a lasting impact and really mean something for millions of poverty-stricken people hoping for a change.

On February 23, Martin took time out to honor one of the men who had meant so very much to him—W.E.B. Du Bois. During a stop in New York, though he was busy meeting with key organizers about campaign tactics, Dr. King participated in a 100th year celebration honoring the memory of Du Bois, whose scholarship and contributions are very

To Honor W.E.B. Du Bois

important in black literature and history.

Martin spoke to an overflow crowd at Carnegie Hall. He praised the scholar's important book, *Black Reconstruction*. Du Bois, more than anyone else, Martin said, "demolished the lies about Negroes in their most important and creative period of history."

Martin began to study the predictions that had been made in the recently released Kerner Commission report, a study of the race riots of the 1960s that had rocked the nation. He was troubled by the findings. He hoped that President Johnson and his administration would do something about racial tension by making new laws to keep the United States from moving "toward two separate societies—one black, one white—separate and unequal." Martin realized that so much more needed to be done.

Now, too, a presidential election was going to take place in November of 1968. Dr. King knew that his choice for a candidate could be meaningful to his many followers. Which candidate would be his choice in the coming presidential election—the current President Johnson, Eugene McCarthy or Robert Kennedy?

Martin delayed revealing his choice, although many believed he liked Kennedy. This made sense, because Dr. King and Robert Kennedy had developed a long-standing relationship. Now, Kennedy was campaigning among the nation's poor and oppressed, supporting the causes of Native Americans, Chicanos, and all minority Americans who were yearning for equal opportunity and a chance to improve their lives. All of this was encouraging for Dr. King as his campaign for the poor began to take shape.

Meanwhile there was further unrest. This time it was in Memphis, Tennessee. The sanitation workers

More Than 15,000 People Showed Up.

there—most of whom were black—had gone on strike after the city refused to recognize their newly formed union and their demands for higher wages and better working conditions. Facing the sticks and clubs of angry policemen, the 1,300 black garbage collectors had been forced to temporarily withdraw. Their next move was to call on Dr. King. Would he be willing to come to Memphis to help them settle a possibly violent showdown?

Martin thought about the request for several days. Then he came to a decision. During his nation-wide tour he would swing through the South in mid-March. He promised to meet with the strikers then.

More than 15,000 people showed up at Mason Temple to hear Martin speak that evening in March. His sermon was as thrilling as any he had ever preached, and the large audience responded in one thunderous chorus after another in their agreement and enthusiasm for Martin's suggestions. As a rally, this gathering was more than organizers expected. But it was only the beginning, Martin said. He promised to return to lead them in a demonstration at the Memphis city hall. Dr. King was not aware that there was bitterness between Memphis's traditional black leadership and the community's young black activists. He had not been told about this split. By the time he returned to Memphis, the feud was near boiling point.

The planned march that day had to be canceled—a surprising spring storm left Memphis under sixteen inches of snow. Martin and other leaders told their supporters that the march would take place the following week.

A few days later Martin received another death threat. His aides were deeply concerned about how disturbing some of these calls were. Some of the

Another Death Threat

callers resorted to cursing. Everyone felt depressed and discouraged—even fearful. Martin spoke about his own possible death, and his people were worried. But he kept to his mission. He firmly believed that his work for civil rights—his presence—was needed here.

When the march was finally about to take place, Martin's problems were mounting. He had arrived late to the march. He had to be rushed by car to the front of the demonstration. It was clear, too, that the march was not well organized.

Martin saw several "Black Power" signs carried by the marchers. The same young militant black activists, who had been a thorn in the side of the city's traditional black community leaders, had promised to disrupt the march if they were not given a key place at the rally.

Martin was at the head of crowd when he heard

the sound of rocks crashing through store windows. In a matter of minutes, a parade of peaceful demonstrators broke apart and grew disorderly and out of control. Now, the police were able to consider the demonstrators as rioters, an excuse to attack them unmercifully and haul them off to jail.

Martin was shocked by this turn of events. It was the first time a demonstration he had led had become so violent. A press conference was called that evening. Martin apologized for the outcome of the march.

He was clearly shaken by the brutality of the police. He also felt that he was personally responsible that some had used the march to express violent behavior.

The following morning he called another press conference. But rather than a timid, apologetic Martin, the press encountered the "lion," according to

The Lion Roared Like Never Before.

Ralph Abernathy. And the lion roared like never before. Martin spoke at length about his belief in nonviolent protest. He was practically on fire with furious indignation. Even the press did not know what to make of Dr. King's completely different attitude.

"Dr. King," one of the reporters stammered, "what happened to you since last night? Have you talked with someone?"

Martin replied. "I have only talked with God."

The unrest in Memphis was still unsettled when Martin left for Atlanta. He needed rest for his body, soul and spirit.

"I can't tell you how good it is to be home," he told Coretta when she greeted him at the door. "I'm so tired."

"Come put your feet up, Martin," Coretta said. "I'll make you some tea. Do you want to talk about it?"

Martin and Coretta sat quietly with their tea as Martin told her everything that had gone wrong in Memphis.

"They can't give up now," Martin said firmly. "They have to understand that! People don't always understand—they don't have to use violence to prove their point, but they have to stick together. If the protesters begin to disagree among themselves, then they will weaken. I must go back there."

"But why to Memphis, Martin?" Coretta asked. "You're so tired. And there's still so much to be done for the Poor People's Campaign."

"I know," Martin said. "But it's the principle of the thing. It's not just the sanitation workers there. It's everywhere. Their cause is our cause. Everyone's cause. Solidarity is what we need to demonstrate."

"What will you do next, Martin?"

Martin Told Her Everything.

MARTIN LUTHER KING, JR.

"We're going to try again. We can't give up now. I have to go back, Coretta."

As always, Martin was being guided by his conscience and his convictions. But it would be in Memphis that Martin Luther King, Jr. would meet his final destiny.

Chapter 9

I've Been to the Mountain Top

When Dr. King returned to Memphis, he was met by two U.S. Marshals who served him with a temporary court order to prevent him from marching. In a counter move, the American Civil Liberties Union hired three lawyers to appear with Martin in Federal court when he challenged the judge's ruling.

At the end of his court hearing, Dr. King met with militant black leaders and promised to help them put together cultural and economic programs for the poor in the city—as long as their protests remained

To Hear Martin Luther King in Person

peaceful, he instructed them.

With this done, Martin looked forward to some rest. He felt that the evening's rally at Mason Temple would be in the capable hands of others.

But this was not to be. The Reverend Abernathy sensed a restlessness in the crowd when he arrived without Martin. He immediately called the motel and explained to Martin what was happening. Without hesitation, the tireless Dr. King agreed to speak at the rally.

It was a dreary evening in Memphis, and a steady rain peppered the city. But this did not discourage the people who wanted to hear Martin Luther King in person. The hall was packed. Reporters were there in large numbers. The Reverend Abernathy's introduction warmed the audience and set the stage for Martin's speech.

Martin seemed tired at first. But by the time he

reached his prophetic conclusion, the powerful Dr. King whom people had come to know moved his audience as never before:

"Well," Martin paused, "I don't know what will happen now. We've got some difficult days ahead. But it really doesn't matter with me now, because I've been to the mountain top. And I don't mind. Like anybody, I would like to live a long life. Longevity has its place. But I'm not concerned about that now.

"I just want to do God's will. And He's allowed me to go to the mountain, and I've looked over, and I've seen the promised land. I may not get there with you.

"But I want you to know tonight that we as a people will get to the promised land. And so I'm happy tonight. I'm not worried about anything. I'm not fearing any man. Mine eyes have seen the glory of

"I've Been to the Mountain Top."

the coming of the Lord. . . . "

Abernathy, like the rest of the crowd, was amazed by Martin's speech. " I had heard him hit high notes before," he has said, "but never higher. The crowd was on its feet, shouting and applauding—even some of the television crew. It was a rare moment in the history of American oratory, something to file along with Washington's Farewell Address and the Gettysburg Address.

"But it was somehow different than those speeches because it was an eloquence that grew out of the black experience, with its similarities to the biblical story of captivity and hard-won freedom. Everyone was emotionally drained by what he had said, including Martin himself, whose eyes were filled with tears."

There is no way to understand completely Martin's moment of prophecy that night. History shows that he was enduring great stress at the time. His tears may have been shed for those who resisted his plans for the Poor People's Campaign; or perhaps for the young militants who had so violently disrupted the first march in Memphis; or for the war in Vietnam; or they may have welled up from the burden of leadership Martin Luther King had chosen to carry on his own shoulders—his mission in life.

Coretta's impressions of her husband's final speech is full of meaning and insight: " So intense was the audience's emotional response to Martin's words," she wrote, "so high was his own exaltation responding to their excitement, the action and reaction of one to the other, that he was overcome; he broke off there. I believe he intended to finish the quotation—'His truth is marching on.' But he could not."

On the following day, April 4, 1968, Coretta

Staff Members Burst In.

recalled, Martin was almost happy, despite his worry about the scheduled march. Moreover, he was relaxed, joking with his brother A.D., and placing a phone call to his mother.

Members of his staff were in good spirits as they met to go over plans for the march, which had been postponed until the following Monday, April 8, 1968. Martin then had lunch with Ralph Abernathy. They shared catfish and salad, eating from the same plate when the waiters failed to bring separate settings.

Martin rested in his room after lunch. His peace and quiet was soon interrupted when staff members burst into his room with the good news that the march had been approved by the judge overseeing the application. Good news though it was, it made no difference to Martin at that point. He had already made up his mind to march no matter what the outcome.

MARTIN LUTHER KING, JR.

Later toward evening, Martin and the Reverend Abernathy freshened up and prepared for dinner. Martin told Abernathy he would wait for him on the balcony. Abernathy recalls that he heard Martin talking to the Reverend Jesse Jackson.

Abernathy was glad to hear the pleasant conversation between the two men, who had earlier expressed differences on several issues. Abernathy listened as the two men talked, Martin on the balcony, and Jesse Jackson below.

"I'll never forget it," Abernathy writes. "I heard a loud crack, and my hands jerked reflexively. It sounded like a backfire from a car, but there was just enough difference to chill my heart. I wheeled, looked out the door, and saw only Martin's feet.

"He was down on the concrete balcony. I bolted out the door and found him there, face up, sprawled and unmoving. Stepping over his frame, I knelt

The Two Men Talked.

down, gathered him in my arms, and began patting him on his left cheek.

"Even at the first glance I could see that a bullet had entered his right cheek, leaving a small hole..."

Abernathy comforted his fallen friend, trying to revive him, trying to understand the words that for a moment, Martin seemed to be trying to say. But a moment later, he was gone. No more words would ever come from the man who had moved so many, and changed America.

After of flurry of activity, an ambulance came and Martin was rushed to St. Joseph's Hospital. At 7:05 P.M. a doctor reported to the Reverend Abernathy and another aide that Dr. King was dead.

When Coretta heard that Martin had been shot, she huddled the children and told them what had happened. With Yolanda's help, Coretta packed her bags and hurried to the airport. She was in the airport when she heard her name echoing over the public address system. Coretta just knew—she knew then that Martin was dead.

Accompanying her was the mayor of Atlanta. He asked her if she wanted to continue on to Memphis, or to return home. Her immediate concern was the children. With tears in her eyes, Coretta wondered how she would tell them what had happened.

"I was afraid that by this time they must have heard—without me beside them," Coretta has said. "But when I got home, Dexter and Bernice had been put to bed, and Bernice was asleep. Yolanda was sitting calmly in the foyer talking on the telephone. Marty was still up, but Yolanda followed me to my bedroom, and she said to me, 'Mommy, I'm not going to cry! I'm just not going to cry, because my daddy's not really dead. He may be physically dead, but his

Tears Flowed Down Yolanda's Cheeks.

spirit will never die, and I'm going to see him again in heaven.'"

Despite her determination not to cry, tears flowed freely down Yolanda's cheeks and she asked her mother if she should hate the man who had killed her father. Coretta explained to her that her father would not want her to do that.

Coretta had very little time to comfort her children. The phone rang continuously and sympathy calls were a constant reminder of her loss. President Johnson and Senator Robert Kennedy were among the officials who offered their condolences. Kennedy volunteered to have a plane available to fly Coretta to Memphis. He also had three phones installed to handle the numerous calls she was now receiving.

Harry Belafonte, a well-known singer and a close friend, called and insisted on staying by Coretta's side to share her sorrow and grief. However, the most touching incident, Coretta has said, was the arrival of Bill Cosby and Robert Culp, then stars of the popular TV show *I Spy*. They came and spent the afternoon playing with the children.

Most of the nation's major cities exploded in fury. Riots erupted in over a hundred places. Washington, D.C. experienced the worst outbreak. More than 700 fires were reported and ten people died. Deaths across the nation soon totaled thirty-nine.

Cities were still disrupted when President Johnson declared April 7 a day of mourning. It was later disclosed that a white man, James Earl Ray, had been arrested. He was tried and convicted for Dr. King's assassination. By 1994, Ray, in prison, was still seeking parole for the murder of Dr. Martin Luther King, Jr.

That following Monday, the Reverend Abernathy and Coretta, with three of her children by her side,

April 7: A Day of Mourning

led nearly 20,000 people in a silent march through the streets of Memphis. Martin was memorialized in Memphis while his body lay in state in Sister's Chapel at Spelman College.

The funeral took place the next day at Ebenezer Baptist Church. The church could hold only 750 of the more than 150,000 people who wanted to attend the services. The turnout was living proof of the broad range of people everywhere, people of every color, who were affected by Martin Luther King's mission and message.

The Reverend Abernathy conducted the funeral which was kept short as Martin had so recently requested in his "mountain top" sermon. At the end of the services, portions of the speech he had given at Ebenezer that February were played. His words, anticipating this moment, were deeply moving—and the nation wept.

MARTIN LUTHER KING, JR.

Martin's casket was drawn through the streets in a plain wagon by a mule train to symbolize the Poor People's Campaign. Thousands of people trailed behind the mule team as it moved from Ebenezer Church to Morehouse College. Even in death, Martin Luther King was leading a march.

120 millon people watched on television. Given its size and the pace of the mules, the funeral procession took quite a while to reach the college. At Morehouse, the president of the college, Benjamin Mays, presided over the ceremony and delivered the eulogy:

"God called the grandson of a slave on his father's side to him, and said to him: 'Martin Luther, speak to America about war and peace; about social justice and racial discrimination; about its obligation to the poor; and about nonviolence as a way of perfecting social change in a world of brutality and war.'"

The Stone Marker

MARTIN LUTHER KING, JR.

Martin was buried at South View Cemetery, near Grandmother Williams.

The words inscribed on the stone marker are those often cited by Martin:

"FREE at last, FREE at last

Thank God Almighty

I'm FREE at last."

Chapter 10

The Legacy of
Martin Luther King, Jr.

Martin may finally have been at peace, but his
family had to carry on. When Coretta arrived home
with the children after the sorrowful day, she had to
turn her attention to their questions and their grief.
Marty told her how much he missed his father.
"Mommy, it just makes me mad that I don't have a
daddy any more," he said sadly.

Coretta assured Marty that in spirit his father
was not dead and would never die. "The thing we

His Family Had to Carry on.

have to think about is how much—even by his death—how much he has helped other people and inspired them; how many people have already said that they are going to help bring about the fulfillment of your daddy's dream." Marty was comforted by the words.

While little Marty slept, the nation mourned the passing of a man who had dedicated his life so that others might be free of racism, discrimination and persecution. One of Martin's most loyal friends, Harry Belafonte, summed up the significance of Martin's life and work:

"When an assassin's bullet ended Martin Luther King's life, it failed in its purpose. More people heard his message in four days than in the twelve years of his preaching. His voice was stilled but his message rang clamorously around the globe.

"Martin Luther King was not a dreamer although

he had a dream. His vision of a society of justice was derived from a stirring reality. Under his leadership millions of black Americans emerged from spiritual imprisonment, from fear, from apathy, and took to the streets to proclaim their freedom.

"The thunder of millions of marching feet preceded the dream. Without these deeds, inspired by his awesome personal courage, the words would merely have woven a fantasy. Martin Luther King, the peaceful warrior, revealed to his people their latent power; nonviolent mass protest, firmly disciplined, enabled them to move against their oppressors in effective and bloodless combat."

Martin's best friend, the Reverend Ralph Abernathy, promised to carry on the work they had started and to complete the mission. "We promise you, Martin, that we will tighten our fellowship and cover our word," Abernathy wrote in his last letter

"We Will Do Our Best."

to Martin. "Don't worry, my friend. We will pull our load. We will do our best. With the help of our friends and above all with the help of God, the Poor People's March will be our first attempt to properly do your will for the poor people of this nation."

The legacy of Martin Luther King, Jr. can be seen in a number of ways. Without Martin's contribution, the civil rights movement then and now would have been far less effective.

Martin was instrumental in bringing the black clergy into the political spotlight, where they continue to have a powerful impact today where social and economic issues are concerned. Martin Luther King stood up for the poor and the locked-out and that legacy has inspired the work of others. King's spirit reaches around the world, affecting any people who have a righteous cause and are prepared to struggle for freedom. This is perhaps Martin's most meaningful and bountiful legacy. Martin Luther King, Jr., will forever be remembered for lighting the way toward peace and freedom for all people.

I Have a Dream

by Martin Luther King (1963)

I am happy to join with you today in what will go down in history as the greatest demonstration for freedom in the history of our nation.

Five score years ago, a great American, in whose symbolic shadow we stand today, signed the Emancipation Proclamation. This momentous decree came as a great beacon light of hope to millions of Negro slaves who had been seared in the flames of withering injustice. It came as a joyous daybreak to end the long night of our captivity.

But one hundred years later, the Negro still is not free; one hundred years later, the life of the Negro is still sadly crippled by the manacles of segregation and the chains of discrimination; one hundred years later, the Negro lives on a lonely island of poverty in the midst of a vast ocean of material prosperity; one hundred years later, the Negro still languishes in the corners of American society and finds himself in exile in his own land.

So we've come here today to dramatize a shameful condition. In a sense we've come to our nation's capital to cash a check. When the architects of our republic wrote the magnificent words of the Constitution and the Declaration of Independence, they were signing a promissory note to which every American was to fall heir. This note was the promise that all men, yes, black men as well as white men, would be guaranteed the unalienable rights of life, liberty and the pursuit of happiness.

It is obvious today that America has defaulted on this promissory note in so far as her citizens of color are concerned. Instead of honoring this sacred obligation, America has given the Negro people a bad check; a check which has come back marked "insufficient funds." We refuse to believe that there are insufficient funds in the great vaults of opportunity of this nation. And so we've come to cash this check, a check that will give us upon demand the riches of freedom and the security of justice.

We have also come to this hallowed spot to remind America of the fierce urgency of now. This is no time to engage in the luxury of cooling off or to take the tranquilizing drug of gradualism. Now is the time to make real the promises of democracy;

"A Reality for All God's Children"

now is the time to rise from the dark and desolate valley of segregation to the sunlit path of racial justice; now is the time to lift our nation from the quicksand of racial injustice to the solid rock of brotherhood; now is the time to make justice a reality for all God's children. It would be fatal for the nation to overlook the urgency of the moment. This sweltering summer of the Negro's legitimate discontent will not pass until there is an invigorating autumn of freedom and equality.

Nineteen sixty-three is not an end, but a beginning. And those who hope that the Negro needed to blow off steam and will now be content, will have a rude awakening if the nation returns to business as usual.

There will be neither rest nor tranquility in America until the Negro is granted his citizenship rights. The whirlwinds of revolt will continue to shake the foundations of our nation until the bright day of justice emerges.

But there is something that I must say to my people who stand on the warm threshold which leads into the palace of justice. In the process of gaining our rightful place we must not be guilty of wrongful deeds.

Let us not seek to justify our thirst for freedom by drinking from the cup of bitterness and hatred. We must forever conduct our struggle on the high plane of dignity and discipline. We must not allow our creative protest to degenerate into physical violence. Again and again we must rise to the majestic heights of meeting physical force with soul force.

The marvelous new militancy which has engulfed the Negro community must not lead us to a distrust of all white people. For many of our white brothers, as evidenced by their presence here today, have

"The Bright Day of Justice"

come to realize that their destiny is tied up with our destiny and they have come to realize that their freedom is inextricably bound to our freedom. This offense we share mounted to storm the battlements of injustice must be carried forth by a biracial army. We cannot walk alone.

And as we walk, we must make the pledge that we shall always march ahead. We cannot turn back. There are those who are asking the devotees of civil rights, "When will you be satisfied?" We can never be satisfied as long as the Negro is the victim of the unspeakable horrors of police brutality.

We can never be satisfied as long as our bodies, heavy with fatigue of travel, cannot gain lodging in the motels of the highways and hotels of the cities. We cannot be satisfied as long as the Negro's basic mobility is from a smaller ghetto to a larger one.

We can never be satisfied as long as our children

are stripped of their selfhood and robbed of their dignity by signs stating "for whites only." We cannot be satisfied as long as a Negro in Mississippi cannot vote and a Negro in New York believes he has nothing for which to vote. No, we are not satisfied, and we will not be satisfied until justice rolls down like waters and righteousness like a mighty stream.

I am not unmindful that some of you come here out of excessive trials and tribulation. Some of you have come fresh from narrow jail cells. Some of you have come from areas where your quest for freedom left you battered by the storms of persecution and staggered by the winds of police brutality. You have been the veterans of creative suffering. Continue to work with the faith that unearned suffering is redemptive.

Go back to Mississippi; go back to Alabama; go back to South Carolina; go back to Georgia; go back

"On the Red Hills of Georgia"

to Louisiana; go back to the slums and ghettos of the northern cities, knowing that somehow this situation can, and will be changed. Let us not wallow in the valley of despair.

So I say to you, my friends, that even though we must face the difficulties of today and tomorrow, I still have a dream. It is a dream deeply rooted in the American dream that one day this nation will rise up and live out the true meaning of its creed—we hold these truths to be self-evident, that all men are created equal.

I have a dream that one day on the red hills of Georgia, sons of former slaves and sons of former slave-owners will be able to sit down together at the table of brotherhood.

I have a dream that one day, even the state of Mississippi, a state sweltering with the heat of injustice, sweltering with the heat of oppression, will be transformed into an oasis of freedom and justice.

I have a dream my four little children will one day live in a nation where they will not be judged by the color of their skin but by the content of their character. I have a dream today!

I have a dream that one day, down in Alabama, with its vicious racists, with its governor having his lips dripping with the words of interposition and nullification, that one day, right there in Alabama, little black boys and black girls will be able to join hands with little white boys and white girls as sisters and brothers. I have a dream today!

I have a dream that one day every valley shall be exalted, every hill and mountain shall be made low, the rough places shall be made plain, and the crooked places shall be made straight and the glory of the Lord will be revealed and all flesh shall see it together.

This is our hope. This is the faith that I shall go back to the South with.

With this faith we will be able to hew out of the mountain of despair a stone of hope. With this faith we will be able to transform the jangling discords of our nation into a beautiful symphony of brotherhood.

With this faith we will be able to work together, to pray together, to struggle together, to go to jail together, to stand up for freedom together, knowing that we will be free one day. This will be the day when all of God's children will be able to sing with new meaning—"my country 'tis of thee, sweet land of liberty; of thee I sing; land where my fathers died, land of the pilgrim's pride; from every mountain side, let freedom ring"—and if America is to be a great nation, this must become true.

So let freedom ring from the prodigious hilltops of New Hampshire.

Let freedom ring from the mighty mountains of New York.

Let freedom ring from the heightening Alleghenies of Pennsylvania.

Let freedom ring from the snow-capped Rockies of Colorado.

Let freedom ring from the curvaceous slopes of California.

But not only that.

Let freedom ring from Stone Mountain in Georgia.

Let freedom ring from Lookout Mountain in Tennessee.

Let freedom ring from every hill and molehill of Mississippi, from every mountainside, let freedom ring.

MARTIN LUTHER KING, JR.

And when we allow freedom to ring, when we let it ring from every village and hamlet, from every state and city, we will able to speed up that day when all of God's children—black men and white men, Jews and Gentiles, Catholics and Protestants—will be able to join hands and to sing in the words of the old Negro spiritual, "Free at last, free at last; Thank God Almighty, we are free at last."